A Move Further South

A Move Further South
By Ruth Garnett

Third World Press
Chicago, Illinois

First Edition 1987 First Printing 1987

ISBN 0-88378-113-1

Manufactured in the United States of America
Third World Press, 7524 S. Cottage Grove Ave., Chicago Il 60619
Production/Design - SERIF, Ltd.

CONTENTS

These are poems of an Afrikan woman who happens to speak English.

That resolved, to you my reader: Power, Blackness, Clarity, Movement, Vision, Life, Love, our Nation.

Thanks to: Dawad, Russell, Raymond, Jimi Israel, Shirley, Quincy, Lynda, Betty, Chris, Saidiyah, Adrienne, Stephen, Haki; and all others who believed.

This collection is for my profoundly loved parents, Irene Thomas White and Freeman Wesley Garnett, who shared with me books, words, and their orbit.

MERGINGS

RITES AFTER VICTORY

So little is left of green grass
On the slopes of these hills
Where we have come to squat and fire clay pots.
The others are all gone; our fathers tell tales
Of spilling the blood of women and infants
Over rock. We took no slaves, all things began new.
There are none of them to shove and move in corners
While our own paramount lives take center stage;
No signs of their hair. Only some night winds
carry sounds of their squared speech and tuneless voices
And only our old ones can hear these sounds
And wince from guilt arising like belches
Of scorched meat. They shake their heads;
There was no other way to go about the settling
Of now ancient questions. No waft of spirits
In breezes bearing music strains, that staved our fear.
We turned the harsh side of our faces
To ensure at least our standing
If not our singing.

Nest season we plant grass
And rains will wash the bloodstains
From the bed of rock and softer earth
Below us. We have divided up our numbers:
The ones with plaited hair are to descend these hills
They will live down there.
We, with our hair in tufts remain
Atop the scalps of trees. We will darken
From the proximate sun, beauty will be named
Our black limbs slashing through the emerald stalks.

The ones below
Will lighten to a color like dried mud
At first, then take on the hue of sandstone
Or light bark. They will be fishermen while we
Hunt game and gather berries from the slopes
To eat our strength, the rest to store in pots
And harbor for the months of feasting
When we will smear our cheeks with clay
And dry them in the sun and head downhill

Toting beads of berries, racks of meat
To give our friends, as they ascend with baskets
Full of fish. They have streaked ash
Ascross their brows, to show that they
Have sanctified our darkness.

Anxious eyes of women
Will confirm the presence of the drums
And blowers of reeds; watching their sons
Whose strides become the drumbeats
Yearly, when we cluster on this terrace
A point halfway.

Else we come again to spilling blood
To despise the lost reflections of our sense
The pale ones; whose voices would become
A shudder in our winds.

We have learned to never turn from music
And the music is our hearts.

HABITAT

I.

We came down from our cliffs
when the ocean parted
revealing the stones swallowed
by time. My love showed to me
the etchings on stone
and was hard like stone.
My eyes became stone

for my next love who also
had sockets of stone. We tossed them
back and forth between us.
I finally dropped mine and ran
before seeing them break
into sand and stuff my footprints.

I ran til another love
caught me. I stopped
to love this time and he
threw stones at me.

We all ran back to the cliffs
where we waited
and had really not left
except in the mind
of our hunger. I saw
all of us there
afraid
of the dance we had

only danced around
each other while the god
blinked but never slept.
He came and strung stones
through my ears
which opened my eyes.

II.

We have moved
without soul
become motionless
perversities
buriers of life.

We have danced idly
not
with deliberation
built tribes.

We have drunk foul waters.
Dysentery
juggled the organs
of our being
til the love god spat at us.

We have fallen
into slime. Where is Afrika
in all this? We have not
searched the question.
Men have become dogs.
I have denounced
my sisters. We
have sung blue songs
made slaves
of love
capital
of our victim.

We have become American.

III.

I am no longer
woman.
I have no hair, skin, eyes
limbs.
I have donned dark cloth
I shrouded skeleton
walk alone
to repeat my shudders.

I join the sea
to find the ancient scrolls
to read the names
of souls who lighted earth.
I climb from waves
speak my own name
to the wind, my hearer.

I am the passion of waves
the coral, pearl and bead
of the sea. Seductress of sun
accomplice to the fertile
jargon of the moon
who calls the seasons of my tides
to harvest.

IV.

The sea, my mother
hardens precious things.
The ocean in me coughs stones.
Come.
Bend.
Read the line of our birth
starburst at our coming.
Keep these stones to know.

Come.
The stones are circled here.
Kiss them, bathe the eyes
for seeing
through the dark
pain of our creation
the sacred
moulding of our flesh.

You
of the same eye
answer my beauty's incantation
our gaze turned

to the same window
where destiny walks by
as infants.

You
who very nearly
killed me
taught that kind
of dying
I am ready
to teach some young child
of life. An old child
of getting past nearer pillars.

The far ones in the distance house the scrolls
and blood has signed my name
to love you
black man
when our spirits rush
down mountains
to the empires of our embrace
ancient
holy as we.

KANEM BY THE RIVER

He has found shoes, laced. Muddied black heap floating
near the bank. His finger tracing the rim of leather
eyes full of what only the mind can touch:

Someone has crossed over.

If anyone should speak, particles will overtake the air.
The soil is a chorus, silent like memory's fist.

Kanem has seen him, one who will not return
to singing. A boat with oars divides
the pewter water. The man dives, swims to it
his teeth clenched to harness any sound.
There is no measure for his breaths.
There was no measure for his pain
like a ceremony, when the firm ground
fell upon his chest, caving muscle and voice.

The one called Kanem among these people
is part god, part man.
The grace of his limbs is of the earth.

His voice is divine, a mastery of their pain.
When the children stumble, it is he
they hear speaking to them.

Kanem speaks what the people do not hear.
He records their terrors, exultations,
what they do not themselves believe.

A deviltry traps these people.
A bizarre and pungent feasting
drains vats of their blood, yet they
affix no numbers to their waste.
These people know no history
except a portion that their minds can bear

which is not enough
to weight down the years that scraped by
with only small space carved for memory:
a rope straining to yield, a body
suspended, an abbreviated sway.

These people love fear more than death.
That is the circumference of their error.

Kanem must tell them now
the soil has buried another shout.
He must salve their fear. They will ask:
What of the chorus ending? The fields
where we groan and drop drive out
our cadences. How is our song to save us?

He will say: The song is in your hearts.
It is a song for hallelujahs
and griefs. Another will pick up
the rhythm for the latest tiller.
Your destroyer is what you do not witness.
You will not peer into its face.

The prophet kneels beside the water
preparing sacred words to show the people
meanings so simple, they do not believe;
and that their life is the death hurtling toward them
that they are now crossing over
and due to their motion, they only seal
the certainty of drowning.

A MOVE FURTHER SOUTH

I wonder how it is their eyes frozen
to beautiful stares, all the while
their feet splayed out into streets
weakened and weaker than
a cow's trolleyed udder; they can go on

and take for this divinity umbrage.
No meat is eaten. No flesh of themselves.

Yet if you beat the Untouchable he will
bleed to death, over dust flooding.

And they make death certain as darkness
and they strangle a segment from dark to light
and no fury is quieted.

To all of us I say who are this segment
estranged by continents and words
we are led to soundless beatings.

And with dust circling
we have not weaved their tapestries
but our flesh into merciless ritual.

And with no honoring of taboo
we have required the siphoning of blood
and the eating of ancestors.

FIVE SONGS

A SURVIVAL STRATEGY FOR DAUGHTERS OF BLACK MEN

Rising
is an act of faith
in shadows
my cries move between. Sometime
I think the day is
a desert
and love is streams.

I often thirst.

For a long
time after you
left your brilliant birds
I clawed flesh
with my cold hands

and moved with chin
lowered
a stiffness of holes
not filled

a long time until
I limbered
enough for love, somersaults
began to see
your holes and my holes
admit light

then understood
necessities of your pain
the corner waiting
for your soul to die
and the pillar
at the center of our house
that needed watering.

When you walked out
sobbing
the walls were strange to me.

The pillar
crumbled. I ate dust

and kept your pain
remembering
your panicked love
when I could have died.
I swallowed
a nickel, calmly.

Hysterical
you held me
while I drank
salt. You held me.
The bones that held
your face
falling
with my retches.

When you caught
me reading
you took away
the sorrow song of Lady Day
and told my heart
do not
go to certain places yet.

I went to all the places
that your love survived.
I learned to see behind screens.

I still have holes
and sweet boys bring
cheese love
where no one anchors.

Love and holes and cheese and dust
one must learn to eat
together
when offered   and also
singly. At table
both hands work together

and in sifting water
for pieces
of rock in the mind's
vault of feathers.

I am there a lot
and my cup runneth over.

Do not be afraid. Wade
in the water.

There is enough to drink.

DOWN SWINGIN
(for all NON-spokespeople)

I am
not crazy   the world I'm
afraid is.

Which oughta
rock your boat
a little bit more than if
twas just me

out here bouncin
off walls
while pigs got me
foamin at the mouth.

I seen way too much
and trouble done found my friends:

Bobby took a needle to his arm
and Adele took that white man
to her bed. Charles and Carver
took that tv   and then
was took to jail.

You say
be like you.
Now listen   you
is ignorant.

Who would mistrust
a poem twists a knife
dully

and I could be loud
about this
but I am not really
that loud

and resent
your ability to transform
my nature
by   obstructing   it.

Evybody talkin bout hebum
ain't going
there.

TEET

This quite down lady
went to Catholic school
but is still really
quite down.

Catch her rap
bout her man
her piana playin
lover man.

Bout how
having class is all in
how/you/do
it. Important info
far as women go.

One afternoon
and after church
Teet sat and ran
it down. When he ain't
wid her he sho wid me
says I cain't
keep nothin from him.

Before my mama died
her words were rubber
and easily snapped

tellin me
a man be like a child
does what he can.
A man does
what he can.

Teet
stopped drinkin
but not before the liquor
beat her down.

Baggage excess
for a music man
I ask her
silent now.
Is half/a man enough
for one whole/woman?

And so much woman
so much
heat
so much
earth
so much
fire
so much
holy water
and
all/that/love

blown
in a fast key.

And
did you get
to all the things you had
to do
for Teet?
Teet.

Teet.

My eyes tell me lookin
where your passion went
from. Thinkin where
it could have
gone.

Spirit
cannot be macked

is goin aroun comin
aroun.

You see
you pay

not for method
but for madness.

RADCLIFFE 1973

Another mush meal
in the ivory tower.
Alta is real and runnin
it down:

"Yeh, I got the trait;

but I damn straight
ain't gon
marry no cracker."

TRUMP

The eyes
the innocence
of plump girls
sisters
whose complexity
is hairbraids

wonder have they heard?
wonder have they heard?

Love
it don't care nothing bout you.
Leave you standin
tremblin like a leaf
maligned by wind.

Love
have you bleedin like a heart
of sunset washes sky.
Easy
to go under
and on out.

Mama now too good for lovin
with that man
not workin
sleep all day.
She told him

Baby
if you here you have to help me
with this livin
beat by air
and these children
(see more evil every day).
I cannot burn your light
and mine.

What you say? You through
with layin out your heart

for its daily tramplin
and your mind
from ragin is a sore;
you can only sleep
like dyin.

That's all I need to know
then out you go.
Babies cannot hear a mother
moan at midnight

Man took everything but memory.

Sometimes
she wants to beg for his return
she
who will give love
but who will not drink
muddy water.

End of summer
catch her
sitting with sternness
in her eye and less light.
Until she will recall
he was the sun
and she the moon in orbit
danced a heated dance
that brought the seasons to flower.

Then she will
rising
gain the doorway where the girls
are sleeping
curled
one by the other's side.

You will be my passion
my belief
my womanness
that stands now blunt.

You must take on
the seeking of this worthy thing
I sought
never minding that the cards
I held were wrong.

I would not deny you harvest
for the sake of drought.
My grapes have rotted
see that yours will turn to wine.

THE HEART'S REGIONS

A REFLECTION ON THE EXIGENCY OF SUCCINCT RESOLUTION

It is
a late hour
night;

I do not need
to make
sense

I need
you.

THE HEART'S REGIONS
(for Saidiyah)

Which gourds are to eat and not leave us to spit
strange fibers? Beauty does not fade a riddle;
it polishes a knife of words we float beneath our shared
roof. The bright scraps of honed loneliness.

Specks bewilder your eye, watching the meek cat's
swelled shanks amble to the rough couch.
No efforts leech her like our worry
under this moonsign. It is not with us like the cat

pressing a nose to see through diaphanous light
a mound behind glass that swells, disappears.
Sadness works your mouth, thrusting down, down
to its cavity. But love is not habit.

Only as a sad mistake. A missighting
of possible glow. A bureaucrat's check
accounting for inventories. It is always bigger
what the world sees, and always small. Rarely heartsap
or the arteries of a gray mound.

I have bitten deep into a staunch rind
hungering for flesh and got flesh
and a torrent defiant of blueprint.
Do not scoop my apertures
seeking implants. They are there

settling as the tile over roughened walkways,
the heart's regions; known to cry out
and to yield title to riches
when issuing no disclaimer to lovers,
frontiersmen.

DEALING SCRAPS

I must have back this breath
you take away
dryly
like wine.

Your love
is formidable, like night
and certain prodding
to sobs.

When you leave
it is with nothing left;
weird shadows
haunt the light
and my gaunt reflection
in glass.

I have lingered
at my neighbor's house
to steal from time
and her sorrows

I seek out strangers.

In my own house
I am stranger
to the thick presence
of your absence.

For these hours
I invent
importances. These thoughts
have pulled all threads.
My mind lies limp.

Your lust carried me
to this trickery
when you racked the crannies of
my woman's heart.

I do not think
I can no longer
make magic.

I have exhausted
patience. Every thing
has drained away

except this desperate love.
except this desperate love.

A CASE IN POINT

I am still
like always when
my mind travels from lunacy.
You are hung. Bones, habit, like old beliefs
are dents where I should have
carressed you. That godliness swapped
for this forfeiture.

Man. Come on now
Man. Be a man. Be my man.
Come back from where you are now
in the waste
land. Things do not
go better with
Coke always. I hear

Your music is lost. They say
in the chamber where
your soul rots. Your woman is fast
so I hear, and what could
you tell your grandmama to her face
who died and left you this life
you let sicken?

This is another one
of those attempts
to roll away the stone, while overlooking
the pebbles one could pick up
and not fall under.
Enough weight knock you down.
I need you to stand, so I can

and cover you sometime.
I didn't know the last time
when I held back, was the last
time, and that I would
come to desire the dead.

You see, the time when I
could not touch, Love
mounted my shoulder

anyway, and you know
fate be tricky sometime
like
she lay a jones on you

so I know about breaking
habits. So if this is
a race, why don't
you win.

TWO LOVE POEMS

You have conquered the land
between their houses.
I am the well that awaits
to drain your tiredness.
I am the couch awaiting you;
to consume what hardnesses
come about you.

A flower I have not seen
is what you have brought me
in this silence. I know its color
of labia, its blood-thirst
for my reading.
I can give it no water
because of this silence.

The tree where underneath
you are bending
has limbs arched from my love;
they do not arrogantly
scrape the sky.
They, like my hands, chafe
to hold your sun-face.

Each time when you come
it is hardier. It lives
from the noise water makes
falling on skin, and the scream
where my loins are. Now my mind paints
a distance of abandoned rhythms.

There are scruples like gems
at an altar of your nurturing.
Who is rightful owner of this offering?
For you, earth beckons and yields its crust.
My breath, spated, is shaped
into pieces like dreams

How you assault this room
and rivet my gaze on this flower
the tenacious growth grafted
where my soul blossoms;
the rock that lodges
in the definite opening of my need.

Lead me from these dead
impoverished entrances, make entrance
to the chamber where my faith is spawned.
Know the things between us
are life and death, are holy moments.
Shore my belief. Lift me from this earth
so I can walk straight in it.

We are public lovers, private strangers.
You want a quiet glamour to refresh
your eyes. My entreaty is the thunder
blasting your arid distances. The world
sprays our speeches to the wind
hurls our vows against storm.

THRESHOLD

I have felt your stiffening
like a forsaken commandment.
At the point of my grief there is
utmost life, an expanse
for your tribe and love.

You, Lover, I do not see
at midnight; but I must know
your rages against the forest
your ramblings among blades
that cut and heal.

I am sure there are stars
out your way, though unable properly
to count them. None are here.
I beg you come battle the sky
which has voided color. You, nor I
cannot resist sunrise.

The distance wedged between us
is a blade. You enter me like knives.
My blood spills out through gashes
numerous as the words forsaking
this moment, departing without breath.

We are in need of speech
to calm this silence, weighted air
that keeps us crawling. Come.
Speak your vow to me. Come.
We are married to the age.

There is nascent language
stitched inside your mouth.
You team at the insides
and have sight like steel under sun.
I sit in your palm, awaiting prayer.

SOME WORDS FOR A SPEECH

I do not know what is tenderer
than truth, or hardier than a lie;
or where famine is
or what victory to seek

or whether there is love among us now
or ever was, in any man's tribe.

As man is steel, so woman is
reflection without glare
or blind alloy. We relinquish our eyes.
Blindness caters to our loins
moreso than sight.

My redundancies are steel.
Heat swarms round this vessel
til it cracks. It is an unsipped feast.
You have bitten my belief and not swallowed.

Below every river is dust.
And whether this thing is the blackest
or less than hard, or unlike a death
I do not say. I do say
I have said enough.

A spring dries up.
Love is an eye closed
to shameless baptismal. I want to see
where you have eaten. I dare you

show me remnants of a meal.

I AM AGAINST THE CEILING AND THE FLOOR

I am against the ceiling and the floor.
We are a sandwich. You block the light
of my questions and scald me. No air
can come through this shroud, your body.
And I, though suffocating, am absent.
Your fucking me like I am not there
accomplishes this.

In this room a table of wood
legs curved and pompous, a beauty
though not the seat of war.
Therefore it stands. I crawl from this
weighted air. You, a man, do not
credit my desperation.

When you go out of here
I will be wearing you. The brass squares
in my ears you sent from somewhere
a time when you could stretch your arms
yeastily, and see your own breaths turn full
joining the mist.

I notice here nothing evaporates.
Everything stays, so that I
cannot lift you.
I weakened when my consonants went stale.

And right now, I do not love you.
Though you have been in all your
divinations, movements, resolute
no reservoir is apparent to me.

And yet, I know you to be wise
leaving behind ornaments made of brass
which tarnishes, seldom breaks.

I HAVE STOLEN YOUR LADDER

I have stolen your ladder.
You hang by fingers of will
onto an edge; there are no grooves.
I can see the testaments of will
combed into rock.

Now I am a bird.
I am flying to you.

ACT TO FOLLOW

Mary, drawing the miracle from Him
Mary, with hair falling down
a rag to cleanse Him. What can I
do to my man that is fission, eon?

It is the age. We seek the perfect love
eluding us. Muddying our feet
we shelter a hollow light of scorching breath.
The dragon is between us.

We want a conquering.
We must bleed as the dragon bleeds.
This want is the only freedom that chains us
under the eyes of wives
under the eyes of the villages in us.

You come to me, words undo me.
What I have to tell you heralds more than mornings
or the gruesome simplicity of a knight.
The true sound of language peels from my lips.
I will see your ears shaved.

You extend me some ground. How I am drawn to you.
There are no boundaries for my seeking
that are thinkable. You have crafted me a box.
There are worlds without.

INTERMENT

If I were close to the soil
of an island like yours
my days would redden,
and foliage take root in my palm.

But I have breathed too long gritty particles.
They overtake the air and fill
violations. All stumble who walk here.

And in the one place beyond all obstacles
an excavation has begun.

P

My thoughts emerge, locusts,
while the years recede. Cambridge
is no place for contradiction.
I loathe these tensions of sleep.

This possibility (of your hunger)
is my hunger, and we both awed.
The years, they warrant that. These moments
are the necessary breaths.

NOCTURNE

Sweet Man, hurt-strong

come
running over night
mares to me groaning.
Joy and pain arrive
together in this night

of veiled magnificent armor.

When sun people dance
do the danger dance
conquering our enemies

when doors beckon to us
where we are lying, call us to walk
against rhythms in particles of fear
and, faltering, stand to lose our movement.

This intersection is our blood. May we know
fondnesses and births and feast
seated with the ancestors.

It is time we knew our coverings
flesh-scent over distances.
We may never know
the hour of our rescue
but the constant face of our rescuer

is us. Listen. For sun cycles
to rage the night. And my voice
shadowing your footfalls.

JUST TO SURVIVE

"Yet we have no idea
why we are struggling here
faced with our every fear
just to survive."

—Scott-Heron

SHOPPING MALL VISION
(for Hoyt Fuller and his vision)

The girl with slick braids
who stands next to some merchant's
candy box reflects
what we will never
approximate
and what exactly
we are

an army of dancers
amazing as the blues we sing.

Her movement
should we wait to see her
undulate air
is the soul in us
plunging its jailed textures
not delicate like teacakes.

Our children's defiled heads
be the sign
of our inadequate growth.

But this poem is not to derogate our struggle

and
the nature of movement
does not matter
as long as we are
constantly moving

with time

a monument.
We bled long
over the steps
while climbing and muttering curses

the way of one choking
from the neglect of neighbors
seen both as pestle
and fellow dust. Identical
to the naked eye and heart
of our sight. The end the pendulum
swings forth and back from.

Always we scream
to have the very reflection
we season our hair to avoid
and our longing is endless
even after millions
have paraded before us
snapping spines
in the stunning
mastery of motion.

We must admit
to despising what we are
when we see it.

But this poem is not to derogate
what we have learned

while barely standing.
We be a shadow
against walls
where the region is inclement
left with nothing to see
without straining.

These dim walls
dictate death to our image
if we do not say
feed me
with these my own eyes
our shout
being utterly necessary
to ready ourselves
for the stoning

the way of silencing
the breath of millions
if we do not hear
with our hearts
and see our own face
enough
to know what to love
and answer back.

We who died before
without eyes
are not afraid to live
out all our textures
and speak to that.
We are
ferreting our need
in this doomed place
too grim for our reflection
where the children are doomed
to the lie planted as history
fed distortion that is madness
led to a playground
of deadly growths.

History is too large
to have accidents
like us
planted here to flower
at the beginning
of the end
as we posit our self
in the storm
constant in our movement

when there is so much to say
we are speechless
but our understanding is deep

like the endurance of rhythms
and postures
signs of life
breeding
dancing up walls.

COMPANION

I cannot walk   into years
without this hurt learns
my pace.

I will walk with it.

I cannot sing
unless to carry the notes
of our sorrow.

This is to be my song.

I cannot eat
without biting the rocks
that layer this terrain of death.

I will eat rocks with fruit.

I am not
one whose memory changes
colors like a season
of leaves falling

as are you
who forget that you have
walked with me
this labyrinth
of love and pain.

You cannot raise
your eyes or move
with shoulders
lowered and back

leaving room to rock your spirit.

It is your soul
I walk to find.
I sing

the resurrection of your spine.
Yours is
the body of my communion

I eat to make you whole again.

You have lost
what you have thrown away:
the scalings from your stumbling
steps   and the shriek
that leaves your mind as
you retrace them.

II.

If you go inside the temple
and find that there are money changers
it is all right to cast them out.
But first, distinguish what is sacred
whether there are doves passed over
to the fattest purse.

If in fact you are not where
you thought yourself to be
whatever is grave, lift it up
to laughter, an honest sound.
I tell you

soon there will be no error
inside your entrances
and you will listen for
and answer only pure callings
and you will see your false steps
woven, strangling themselves.

III.

Let us hope this land divides.
Let us hope your spirits are then dead.
Your deaths will not then be on our hands.

We will salvage your children, if we can.

Each day enacts destiny.
Each morning is crisp, though different.
The danger of sacrifice is the avoidance of it.
What is consumed is what is most valued.

But you do not hear.
You do not read, in order that
you cannot remember
and so that everything stays the same.
I give a warning to you, Malcolm's:
In China, the children spilled your blood.

This legacy of the house
constitutes no renewal, no vision
called forth; you will perish
when colors will not pry the scab from
your eyes.

All this is clear.
We will salvage your children, if we can.

GRENADA POEM

Some things cannot be art, Maurice,
like the way blood flowed from their eyes.

A poet woman grieves for you
to come to us, your strong walk
carrying you. Of all things

they planned your death;
an evil perfect like sculpture.

My people grabbed onto an edge,
migrationing. We came dead center
here where your daughter
birthed Malcolm; this desert now,
in that it declares an absence.
The lies made easy by foliage
covering our dead.

But there are tongues not coiled.

There is one word my heart speaks.
Grenada.
I have but one breast to feed into
the mouth of this soil.
There is but one name I can name myself.
Uhuru.

And here are words to rekindle the land:

When blood is drunk in the presence of animals
one cannot be too careful. In full view of enemies
one cannot look the other way.

AFTER LEVELLING
(for Stephen)

You ask now for words
of Malcolm. Here, the edifice still stands
though the young men roll away downhill.
Hasten, for you have not witnessed.

And you have not seen
the rivers I would heave
from the blossoming of my tears
to cradle Malcolm's bludgeoned head;
to hear unwavering his voice, saying

Come, Brother. There is no need to fear
the destruction of what we seek.
We are each others' hands.
Get to that.

Your manhood salutes me
where I stood gazing at my own
splintered belief. This poem
for you my brother and our struggle
are your reflection. Mirrors disintegrate;
and we are not quite sure
which wind carries us
the way of currents spawning life.

There is darkness on the water
eating alive so many
and the terrible witness
making stone of the rest.

Speak now while my voice drowns
and I will surface and speak shields.
There is no voice in hearing
but I have heard one
paddle the death stillnesses.

I hail you
swimming towards an echo
on the other side. A tree

awaits the coming of your strong tribe
and freshwater.

NATALIA KANEM
(for Walter Rodney)

This new name you have is impeccable;
a summary. Heavier than I thought
a mere symbol could be.

Yet, as we sought what hallows us
far from your sun country and my home
the heart of hell; drank the blueberry leaves
foreign to St. Louis, where the gospels I have
are muffled by the pounding of my heart
we were fragmentary, plodding.

Now there is a country grown inside
your smooth, consistent belly.

And I am glad for you
and for this child
to know a generosity only beauty
can reach. And I remember your old names
and your sorrowing for your friend
who named you last.

And as they shot down twilight
they would not think of our obsession:
this loss. And each new season
a womanhood semester, leading softly
to a fondness for guns.

DORSALS

I. What The Lovers Said

This discourse makes no inroads.
We ogle the dark in our lives
like insufficient metaphor.

We look at action that precedes speech;
as cumbersome as babes
ridiculous as the old.

II. The Auction Block

These moments we do not salvage
are sold away from us like once
destiny was in curled bits of flesh.

The years have rendered me
blind skeleton. My teeth close around
an emptied loaf.

III. The Young Woman, Unmarried, Childless

Some of the children will
be clean-faced and strong
and know the current of love
and will not wish to swim against it.
Some of the children will be strong
enough to shoulder love's vessel
enough to drink from it.

IV. Dorsals

We have put our backs to dowries
thrown gifts behind a net.
We see as those who live always
behind the net.

They have been leeches on
our ribbons and our Sundays
seen our lips
and wanted to own our laughter.

In front of the net we have been
waiting for unblurred lines.

But find only remnants sent
by our hearts, when we will thirst
and drink them as words; be led within
a quilt that is our lives
to histories grafted like
the colors of our hands when we are linked
in patterns costly as the love
we left for plundering
among scraps
of our beauty now skinned
alive. There have always been
butchers present. It is a matter now

of saving skins and rightful coverings
retrieval of gift and garment, guarding
eyesores and the hungers of the beast.

IN BEDFORD-STUYVESANT

POEM FOR NOW

It is harder to make small movements
and live minutely.   I too
wish to be part of this dance
but mend my costume apart.

Spirit is also unseen
and not immediately clear.

In flowering I almost
choked on a seed   one time
but now barely remember. Things
are at a point of questions. I know
I am out of

sync   for instance
I cannot answer where my children are.
But let me just

say in my defense

freedom's not an easy birth
and labor is always
hardest the first time. I try
to do what is necessary   but then
my necessities are few

like love
will make me bend
and the places I keep
going back to and the truth
that comes to light.
I am well aware of

children peering through dark windows
where decaying ones plan their death.

SPRING SISTER SONG

A nail crucifies this wall.
I hang dead center the oil.
Two men are singing; old men
during slavery time. Maybe not called
men, but the song proving it for them
the two and for us who are millions.

My sister bought and framed
this canvas for me one frantic holiday.
It is a gift like wood
a bond between leaves;
though she will not always
say she is one of us.

I say it, the song proving it.
On holidays I think of her
and all things that matter.
Death. The last scion
of any song. Festival for which
we all are celebrants.

The layers of paint swathing
this wall are old names for colors.
I must remember to seek
nails straining in plaster
like visions carping the heart.

The day is ornate with metal.
Old men are dead and singing to me.

LEAVING BED-STUY

She didn't have no roaches or no lights, and was a boy-man. Filthy, too. The man said all that, packed a giant metal bullet and climbed the stairs to do his poisoning. He is a handsome man, though old and given to spite. Or maybe, it is just strong preference.

Though he maligns the woman that lived here before, and condescends to Ms. Thomas who is also old, still he likes me. He is from some Southern somewhere and is warm and smiling when he comes and wants to hug me, though I believe this an innocent gesture, if any man has innocence.

The other women in this house also bear the scrutiny of this miniature Southern man; and of this stately house harboring our misshapen days.

Minnie, broad Carolina back, small red-kerchiefed head; loud. Ambling in and out for gossip with other women who fan in front of brownstones, once the heat announces itself like a guest we are obliged to board each season.

Minnie, wary of me, but calming when she sees a man out front with me, any man. She likes the poet with the curly hair. This is for her comfortable obsession, exigency of my migration here. As if, otherwise, she becomes an oddity to herself, perusing me. She would have men now if she could, a man kept away from her heated confidantes.

The woman with my name coming home drunk, halted by the staircase, stern, appraising her. She must reach the top where her son, who is retarded and graying, awaits, bellowing out her name. His voice must pull her up each stair, some strange, inverted umbilical, calling her name and my name over and over. Sometimes I look out at her stupor. She tells me once, having passed her own stool onto her ankle: I did this to myself. It is not mud. Just to indicate she is clear.

Ms. Thomas has said this woman was a proper lady once, before her husband died. She started drinking then, his eyes no longer upon her. I wonder about the woman's own crusty eyes, what blindness has occurred to them.

Ms. Thomas has deep deep eyes in her smooth face and proud Baian[1] skull, is clean and kind, and lonely enough to tell me of the father she escaped; the domineering man insulting her small frame and large energy. Once she had gained weight. "It looked good on me." She is happy that I am clean and an early riser.

Our exterminator finishes and leaves, this time he does not knock again on my door. He is quite emotional. He seems to want mothering. I am not old enough to mother an old man.

Ms. Thomas and I love this house, her house. I scrub the linoleum to perfection. On the bare terrace, I never plant jonquils, gladiolas and collards, but keep on reading the gardening book.

Often he is here, the poet. Wherever Trinidad is, it carries a pulse of my flesh to its mouth; and I hear this voice. Wherever I am.

There are tall ceilings, large windows front and back, white walls, my books

to terrorize me when I am too full to write. My students papers strewn like leaves. My dread in this chaos of returning them.

And I am baking bread because the poem won't speak to me.

Bomani coming here and bringing words, incredible words, and his huge hunger for fruit. Our bond this staggering war. And the other poets sitting on my couch. Lemon and salt will bleed rust from fabric on upholstery; that is how I saved it.

Books and china behind glass. Our talk that makes this work crystal or sand.

---

[1]A native of Barbados, a Caribbean island.

Bed-Stuy is urgent and crisp in sun. Assata somewhere hiding. I do not dress in the Western mode here. Women who are respected on the street are wrapped in kinte, longer skirts.

There is a junkie, Cantrell, who helped us boycott the Arabs. They had struck him with a machete as they had done others. We hate them for fondling little girls and also boys.

Napoleon was in prison seven years. They have hurt me all they can, he tells me. There is no need for you all to walk here in front of them carrying signs. I can destroy them all in a matter of seconds. Just come by the florist's. He is my godfather. Leave a message for me there.

He has walked me down to the end of the block where I turn and go up home. We have passed the shooting gallery the city will not brick up. Some of us want to send Dobermans in there, where the junkies leave the curtains parted, and it is summer and hot, and their lights are on.

Where would we get dogs, what if the junkies have guns, what if the police arrest us? How does idea become action?

I turn up the block leaving Napoleon and his idea. It has bitten me worse than a Doberman ever could. I come back out to the street and call Bomani:

I am outside. There is a man here who wants to kill the Arabs, early in the morning before our picket line forms. We get there at 7. He would come before and disappear like a shadow into the street.

Bomani tells me: We must struggle in all ways. Decide what is safe and best for you to do.

We say goodbye. I am shaking. My mind is firm. I know what is best for us to do. Nothing is safe.

In Austin, there are shops and people that sparkle with the accumulated crystal of fulfilled whims, their heirloom and birthright. My sister and I sit across from her friend, who has thick thick hair. This woman's sister also is a writer; the four of us, oddly, a matched set.

We are all survivors. I am proud of my sister, these women, the four of us, our black firmness, our staunch minds and ancient beauty, among these whites. We are not guaranteed what they have settled for: milk punch; croissants; jam; sterling. We have survived our appetites. We have survived guarantees.

My sister and this woman have married well, have children. The writer, married once, childless. Me, neither engagement. The writer and I when we meet talk and talk, my sister's friends, doctors, lawyers, students, around us. I love the writer out of a deep deep place. She is my island in this gathering. We are treetall women battling with words. We know. We articulate.

I love my sister, bringing what magic to me, she does not know; her children ripen me. I am often dry earth; she is reservoir.

I do not call Napoleon. The brothers convince me they can negotiate. They have had talks with the PLO.

I tell them, but Beirut is being bombed. This is Bed-Stuy. We are in Brooklyn.

The men say I am stubborn. I have no battlescars. Later, someone says I am an agent.

Mutima saves me from hurtling my rage: Write for our paper. I want to write about Assata, Accoli, Bilal, Fulani, the traitor at the trial. I want to interview their organization. We are afraid of agents and the FBI.

And so death traps us while we are alive. And what is death? I ride the train. Three youths stand opposite me.

I could carve up that ass in two seconds flat. Old yella bitch. I hate muthafuckin bitches like that. Just like I cut that other nigger, I could cut her up.

I am reading the NY Times Book Review. Can you read, I start to say to them. I am determined, if they touch me, I will show no fear. I will not die like this. I will tell them that Arabs are maiming other brothers like them, fondling their sisters' breasts before they are 10. Go to Fulton Street and carve up some Arabs. Go to Crown Heights or Flatbush. There are thousands of them everywhere.

I read about Norman Mailer's Egyptian novel. I could carve up his ass in two seconds flat.

Past my stop, I am on the street where Eubie Blake lived and has just died.

It is a holy street. I take holy steps. My mind comes back from everywhere, so I can pack and leave Bed-Stuy, becoming its ancestor.